the LENS to HOPE and JOY

find, see, and become grace,

Marcia Fackler

marcia fackler

Fedd Books
P.O. Box 341973
Austin, TX 78734

www.thefeddagency.com

Published in association with The Fedd Agency, Inc., a literary agency.

ISBN: 978-1-957616-76-6

LCCN: 2024937193

Printed in the United States of America

Dedication

This book is the story of a miraculous shift of mind that occurred by changing focus and looking through a new lens. There were two parts to my journey, outer and inner. The story is dedicated to those that guided both.

First, to the non-profit organization, Dress for Success Louisville, that guided me on traveling the outer road. Being involved with this organization allowed me to find and see hope through witnessing an abundance of compassion, goodness, and success.

Secondly, the story is dedicated to the wise teachers and authors I have quoted that guided me on the second leg, the inner journey. They led me to insights and knowledge that inspired contemplative thought. This inner work routed me through my cynical, fearful mind to find my hopeful, joy-filled soul.

Contents

Two Wolves

An elderly Cherokee chief took his grandchildren into the forest and sat them down and said to them, "A fight is going on inside of me. It is a terrible fight between two wolves. One is the wolf of fear, hatred, anger, selfishness, self-pity, and lack. The other is the wolf of love, compassion, humility, gratitude, kindness, hope, and joy."

The children were very quiet and listening attentively to their grandfather. He then said, "This same fight between two wolves that is going on inside of me is going on inside of you and every other person."

They thought about it for a minute and then one child asked the chief, "Grandfather, which wolf will win?"

He said quietly, "The one you feed."

Once upon a time, there was an ordinary woman with an ordinary life and ordinary fears. The big, bad wolf of fear that lived in her mind became very hungry. She kept feeding that hungry wolf, and he was growing bigger and bigger. The bigger he got, the more he needed. She felt like an endless source of fear and anxiety, and it seemed this wolf had taken over and found a bountiful place to live. She became so tired and wondered how she could go on feeding this hungry wolf.

Still, the wolf of love was gently whispering to her through the fearful chatter. She heard an invitation to join him on a journey. She could also hear her mother's wise words: "The mind is like a book; it only works when it is open." So she decided to open her mind and heart, and she followed this invitation from the wolf of love and experienced a miracle.

This little book is the shortened, condensed story of her journey. The story recounts how she came to stop focusing on mostly what was wrong with her life and the world but instead finding and focusing on what is right with her life and the world. You might say she began to see through rose-colored glasses.

In the best-selling book *A Return to Love; Reflections on the*

Principles of a Course in Miracles, author Marianne Williamson defines a miracle as a "shift in perception." As this frightened woman in our story began to change her thoughts and focus, love poured in and began to fill her open mind and heart. She felt her whole world shift and change. She soon realized what a miraculous journey it was. Rose-colored glasses became her symbol to trigger her mind and remind her of the bright lens through which to see. This shift is not a simple, easy task for the human mind to accomplish, and the symbol proved to be an essential part of keeping her on course—a constant reminder. When faced with a challenge, she would both literally and figuratively put them on to change her focus from the negative to the positive, from curse to blessings, from fear to love, from hell to heaven, and from pity to power. She was amazed at how that would transform a situation! She realized that anyone and everyone has this same power in their mind to shift their focus and experience this miracle, so she wanted to share it with others. Because as the wise, elderly chief explained to his grandchildren in the parable, the fight between two wolves is going on inside all of us.

As you may have guessed by now, I am that ordinary

woman in the story and the author of this book. I stumbled upon an effective symbol to quiet the wolf of fear and nourish the wolf of love. Since the beginning of mankind, humans have used symbols to communicate. Symbols hold power, drive actions, and contain emotions that are attached and stirred. I have always possessed a practical, simple nature. My path led me to create, cultivate, and rely on this symbol to guide me when faced with bumps and forks in the road. All journeys contain bumps and forks, and this produces what could be a constant obstacle. The symbol of the rose-colored glasses became a lens that brightened my life and the world around me. It became a lens to recognize and see love, hope, grace, and God and his miracles. Because now that I could see all these things, it was the lens that led me to hope and joy! It was as if seeing things through this new lens was acting as 3D glasses that enhanced the breadth and depth perception of God and life, and all that is good was leaping at me from the screen. I built a trust in the perspective the lens was giving me because I came to believe that it was bringing to focus the hope you can find when you look for and see God in all things.

The Search For God

"The secret to joy is to keep seeking God
where we doubt he is."

Ann Voskamp

I grew up Catholic and treasure the Catholic cultures and traditions that shaped me and taught me. Later in life, I came to see religion as a culture developed around an institution. These faith traditions and cultures originated from a set of beliefs that are based on man's interpretations, sometimes from thousands of years ago. I am not saying this is bad. But it can be limiting and create a barrier to all that these interpreted words have to offer. My religion gave me a strong moral foundation and served me well. It gave me a sense of belonging, and I have fond memories from those traditions. From an early age, I learned and memorized through catechism the concept of God. Some religions evolve, adapt, and mature as more depth is uncovered from these interpretations of man. These religions can offer a wonderful sense of community, support, and opportunity to come together, serve, and learn from each other. Compassionate, nurturing churches frequently offer outreach to lift, serve, and better their communities. When you participate, you experience connections and celebrate these shared beliefs and teachings. This community participation can be like a supportive family and a great benefit.

As an adult and parent, when life got hard and I went looking for answers and purpose, I expanded outside of this set of beliefs and interpretations into what I can only describe as deep spiritual travel through many different realms without religious boundaries. It was an inner journey. This journey took me beyond the boundaries of the beliefs that can divide us and make us different, to find and see our sameness—what connects us. It was an exploration of universal spiritual practices that brought me to a connection to all that is.

Through my journey, I came to ponder and realize that this was also the "way" and the message that Jesus Christ lived. Somehow, through man's mind and fears, some religions, as they were developing, may have overlooked this all important universal, unconditional connection through love. Some religions set conditions for acceptance and participation that Jesus never did. The message was twisted and shaped through man's eyes. Man's fears and prejudices were woven into the fabric of the interpretations. I found that the rigid beliefs and judgments that can be present in religions were confining, limiting, and shrinking God's love. These judgments were stopping the flow and disconnecting me from God. I found more freedom in God's love and found more ways to love. Fr. Richard Rohr, author and founder of The Center for Action and Contemplation (CAC) in Albuquerque, New Mexico, is quoted as saying "Most of us were taught that God would love us if and when we change. In fact, God loves you so that you can change. It is the inherent experience of love that becomes the engine of change."

Through my spiritual travels and inner journey, the learned concept of God turned into an ability to feel and experience the spirit of God, the infinite love of God, and the grace of

God. I developed a friendship with God. This God became a constant companion, and I felt an infinite communion. What I found in expanding my mind outside of this one set of beliefs is that maybe God is too big to contain into one set of man's beliefs and attempts to define—too big to fit into one set of interpretations of this life force. I also learned there is so much that cannot be explained, that man cannot wrap their head around. There is so much mystery, awe, and wonder.

This spiritual searching took me outside the boundaries of my religion, stretched and enlarged it, and then brought me back. I believe that this searching expanded my Catholic faith by going so much deeper into the mysteries of life and opening new paths to God. I still participate in the Catholic mass and sacraments, and, because of this journey, I receive much more from them than I did in the past. But the certainty for me in all that I explored and studied was that God is love, no matter how you title or refer to this powerful energy. This new lens that my journey presented me with allowed me to feel and see God and love in all things.

"For even as love crowns you so shall he crucify you. Even as he is for your growth, so he is for your pruning." These words are from a poem in the book *The Prophet*, published in 1923. The author, Kahlil Gibran, was a poet, philosopher, and artist born in Lebanon. The title of this poem is "On Love." I interpret that he is using the word "love" in the same context as being God because, again, my path directed me to believe that this one word is the only word to describe this boundless God. I believe this wise philosopher and deep thinker uncovered that God was in the joy and God was in the pain. He is "filling us in" on this realization because he knows it is so difficult to find God in our pain. This poem goes on to say: "All these things shall love do unto you that you may know the secrets of your heart, and in that knowledge become a fragment of life's heart." This spoke to me, sending the message that through our pain and fears, through a crucifixion, love and God are there. If looked at as an opportunity for growth, for pruning, a transformation can occur. This transformation occurs by leading you to "the secrets of your heart." That secret that your heart holds could be that love lives in your heart all the time no matter what and is waiting to be brought forth, sometimes through joy (crowns you) and sometimes through pain (so shall he crucify you). If the pain is used for growth, you gain knowledge, you become wiser. This wisdom brings you closer to your connection with your soul and your God. When you can feel this connection, you become a "fragment of life's heart." The pain can bring you to wisdom, and the wisdom brings you to the realization that you are a significant part and a pulse of the heartbeat of the world. You recognize that you are this love that is always in your heart.

This newfound realization, if absorbed, is that God, love, and hope may not be in plain sight and can be hiding. There is a bright lens that is available in your thoughts. When your thoughts are aware of this lens, you can choose to look through this lens. Then, you have chosen to bring God, love and hope to focus on all things and on all people.

> "May the God of hope fill you with all joy
> and peace as you trust in him so that you may
> overflow with hope by the power of the Holy
> Spirit." - Romans 15:13

The God of hope exposed this new lens to me, and with it, laid out this choice. The choice to look through the bright lens led me to see the overflow of hope, which gave me peace and filled me with joy! To get there, I followed the invitation from the wolf of love from the parable, or you could say the power of the Holy Spirit from the Romans 15:13 Bible verse. I just know I was being led by a force on a journey that transformed my life. This journey began in a hell. A hell in my mind, self-created by my pessimistic thoughts and focusing on my fears.

The Hell

> **"The mind is its own place and in itself, can make a heaven of hell, a hell of heaven."**
>
> 17th Century English Poet - John Melton

It is in our DNA to feel fear. We are born with a fight or flight response built into our brains. This response is defined by psychologytools.com as "an automatic physiological reaction to an event that is perceived as stressful or frightening." How much of our precious limited time here on earth is spent living through a "perceived" fear that robs us of the joy we were meant to experience? To quote Mark Twain: "I've had a lot of worries in my life, most of which never happened." Through-out the centuries, much of our governments, politics, and religions have come from a place of fear. Add to those consistent, powerful influences the current 24-hour-a-day news, media, and marketing that are often centered on fear, it is understandable that many in our culture are stressed, anxious, and depressed.

Dr. Dan Baker, PhD., author and founding director of the Life Enhancement Program at Canyon Ranch, located outside of Tucson, Arizona, studies the science of happiness. In his book *What Happy People Know*, he explains that this fight or flight response was needed early in our evolution for survival. Those of us fortunate to be living in first-world countries are no longer hunting for our food or in physical danger from prey or enemies. But, Dr. Baker explains, our DNA still perceives that we are. In today's modern world, this fear and fight or flight response connected to it actually hinders your survival. It cripples us emotionally and fills us with stress, which causes dis-ease. It can suck the life right out of us and darken our weary spirits. We create our hell.

There was a time in my life when I experienced and created a hell in my mind. When I look back now, I wonder, "What was I thinking?!" At one time, my four children were all teenagers and life was chaotic for sure. My continuous loop of thoughts was focused on mistakes of the past and fears for the future. This was creating more chaos and leaving me frazzled, anxious, and distressed. There were schedule stresses, teenager stresses, financial stresses, and what-was-going-on-in-the-world stresses! I felt the world was going to hell in a handbag. It seemed most of my attention and focus was on the negative and what was wrong with my life and the world. I was at war with that wolf of fear—a one woman army battling the world. And the world and the wolf were winning.

This stress is what brought me to my deep spiritual search. This search took me on a discovery journey that turned my world upside down from everything I thought reality and life to be. I came to realize that my choice of thoughts was creating my reality. Even better, I came to realize the power was there in my mind to choose different thoughts. My mind, in its own place, was creating the hell I was experiencing. And I was missing the heaven that was right there if only I could bring it into focus and feed and nurture it.

Finding Heaven

"There's a heaven on earth that so few ever find, though the map's in your soul and the road's in your mind."

Dan Fogelberg

About that same time as my mind began to open and the spiritual searching ensued, I was watching a report on television that sparked a calling to assist in opening a non-profit affiliate in my hometown that served struggling and unemployed women. A short phone call was made, and a meeting was scheduled. Shortly thereafter, the doors were opened, and the journey began. This non-profit organization served struggling and unemployed women by providing interview clothing, job training, resources, and support. This strong support system empowered these women to transform their lives. Little did I know the experience of being involved would also play a role in transforming mine. There were multiple parts to this story that I began to choose to focus on. These parts produced numerous roads that all led me to finding and experiencing heaven.

Through the involvement of this non-profit organization, Dress for Success Louisville, I witnessed so much hope through actions of love, service, and compassion. I saw single moms overcoming addictions, retaining jobs and rebuilding their lives and their families. I saw women who were in abusive relationships leave those relationships, become empowered to succeed, and stand on their own two feet. I saw women who were homeless become financially skilled and independent. This empowered them to buy a home and give their children stability. Even with all the support, none of this was easy for them. We didn't fix them. We offered direction and guidance so they could control their destiny. They did the fixing. They were determined, doing hard things and facing each day with courage and conviction. This was one part. People who were in dire circumstances were transforming those circumstances and were met with an abundance of support to accomplish this feat. Dress for Success Louisville is an affiliate of Dress for Success Worldwide and partners with many other non-profits, so I was exposed to many other organizations with strong missions, doing life changing work and lifting people in need. And, with the worldwide reach, I realized this effect is global. This part led me to see and believe in success and hope.

Another part I was experiencing and choosing to put my focus on was the abundance of willing volunteers coming forward and their selfless, big hearts. Some who were coming forward wanted to help because they had been in the same shoes of the struggling women and knew what they were going through. They understood what it was like to need support. And they understood the overwhelming relief and benefit of being met with kindness and support. Others who were coming forward just had it in their hearts to help and wanted to make a profound difference in someone's life. I was in awe of strong, caring women and men giving so much of themselves, carving out time from their very busy lives to help another struggling human. People were giving their time and donating clothes and money for the cause. These volunteers met the organization's clients at their pain, felt their pain, and shared their pain. Compassion was at work, and hope was in full swing. I witnessed so much kindness.

And, because I began to focus on these things and be more aware, I began to see them outside of the work we were doing within the organization. I was seeing this goodness in people, seeing hope and success happen all around me. I was learning and experiencing firsthand that what you focus on expands. My eyes were looking in a whole new direction and mingling what I was seeing with my thoughts of hope and goodness. I was seeing things completely different from the previous stance that the world was going to hell in a handbag. A whole new perspective grew, a whole new lens filtering and directing my thoughts. This lens was centering a bright light in what was previously focused on much darkness. It was a bright lens!

My thoughts became my prayer of hope and gratitude for all I was observing rather than a source for inciting my fears. They became a source for good. They were a wondrous melody of beautiful notes strumming through my mind. Once I realized I could hum this song and change my tune, my life was forever different. My attention and focus were dominated by productive, hopeful thoughts that sent my soul soaring and brought me to a state of amazing grace. The wolf of love was feasting, and my thoughts were providing wholesome nourishment.

The more I fed the wolf of love, the more he grew and the brighter the world looked. I saw and found the goodness and love that had been blocked by fear and pessimism. The war with the wolf of fear and the world was over, and I won! The world didn't change, but mine did because what I looked for and saw in it changed. My mind was traveling along the road to heaven and leading me to the map in my soul.

Heaven Found

"Heaven on earth is a choice we must make, not a place we must find."

Dr. Wayne Dyer

I came to realize there is good news and so many people working hard to solve our challenges. I saw and met them firsthand. This good news just isn't reported as often or brought to our awareness enough. Changing our lens does not mean ignoring or turning a blind eye to the negative. We all know the world has extremely serious issues and that evil and injustices exist. I'm not saying we should stick our heads in the sand

and pretend that bad things aren't happening, but I found the information we receive is way out of balance. *The bright lens puts focus on following or creating a positive solution, knows and believes there is one, and is fully aware of the love contained in the power of the human spirit.* This is often shown in the face of extreme tragedies in our society, whether human induced or natural disasters. This power and love in the human spirit appears and pours out, sometimes from all over the world. This love that pours out is sometimes the only thing that can bring any comfort. When this happens, it has the potential to soften the tragedy. The people experiencing the devastation don't know how they would have gotten through the situation without the outpouring of love.

Fr. Richard Rohr states "the best criticism of the bad is the practice of the good." One of the core principles of the Center for Action and Contemplation is "oppositional energy only creates more of the same." What you focus on expands and goes in both directions. News brings to our attention the problems, but maybe we feel so hopeless because that is where it stops. The solutions and good practices are there, but I realized that I had to open my eyes, heart, and mind to see it and go looking for it myself. It was a wonderful and adventurous hunt!

Once my mind was newly focused on what was right with the world, that positive energy began to flow into all aspects of my life. In every challenging situation that touched any part of my life, I began to look for a positive perspective. I would ask myself, "How can I make this for good?" I came to choose to see the turmoil as an intended lesson and an opportunity for growth, an opportunity for pruning, that would lead me to "the secrets of my heart." The first step that was needed was acceptance—acknowledging what is happening and recognizing where I am. Carl Jung, the great Swiss psychiatrist is quoted as saying, "We cannot change anything until we accept it. Condemnation does not liberate; it oppresses." When you incessantly condemn a situation, all the attention is going to what is wrong, and it expands what is wrong. This fills you with hopelessness, anger, and fear. How can you get to a place to find answers or direction through anger and fear? They dominate. I found I could figuratively put on the glasses to trigger my thoughts, whip my mind into gear, like a glass of cold water thrown in my face to wake me up. This would remind me to change my lens, not see it in a negative way, and look deeper for the lesson that was hidden in the challenge. Look for where it might lead me. Turmoil pushes and tests you. If you work with it rather than against it, you will find the gift of growth that is wrapped inside. With each new challenge you are then better equipped and ready to take it on. You gain wisdom, become empowered, and this empowerment builds strength and gives you confidence.

Another road that led me to heaven through this non-profit organization, Dress for Success Louisville, was how it expanded my world. It connected me to those who were different from me, and I from them. We have tendencies to create and live in bubbles. Where we live, work, learn, play, and worship can be limited by geography. Bubbles are clear, and we can see out, but they still limit and contain us. This popped mine and took me outside of it. I learned through the relationships that were built with clients from the non-profit that we may look different and live differently, but our deeper wants and needs are very similar. I saw and could feel that we are all more connected than separated. The experiences of these connections felt like a repeated encounter with the sacred—a holy encounter, an encounter with God. Two people connecting through one's pain at a deep level, both giving and both receiving. You could feel their hope rising and their extinguished light begin to flicker. Love was flowing. My hopeful thoughts were that it was felt on both sides of the encounter, and I could feel that it was. *That is heaven.*

All of this led me to become aware and conscious of my thoughts. Eastern faith traditions describe this as an awakening, an enlightenment. I was working to interrupt and program my thoughts rather than allow the compulsive thinking that was controlling me. I used the symbol of the bright lens to trigger my brain and rewire my thoughts when they were not serving me well. I would put those glasses on, and when I could see a situation differently, I could think about it differently. If I was thinking negatively, I tried to get to the source of why. I would ask myself: *was it a repeated pattern programmed in my brain from a past experience that I needed to recognize and overcome?* When we have thought about and reacted to situations in a certain way for years, this repeated pattern is an extremely difficult challenge to break. For instance, my reaction to troubling situations programmed in my brain was usually to label them as bad, to condemn them and complain. This would take me straight to fear. The incessant condemnation and complaining put more focus on and expanded the trouble. My mind would be closed and locked. Guidance, growth, and answers could not break through.

Or was it my own mistrust or lack of confidence? Was it my fears, determined to be fed, not giving up and trying to sneak back in? In my spiritual searching, I learned this was my "ego," what Thomas Merton, a Trappist Monk, activist, and mystic, referred to as the "false self." Eckhart Tolle, a spiritual teacher and author, defines the ego as "a false sense of self that you identify with." When you develop an awareness of your thoughts and go deeper to the realization of why you are thinking them, this is what Thomas Merton refers to as the "true self." You have uncovered your spirit, your soul, and your connection to God. By beginning to go deeper to asking reflective 'whys' to understand your thoughts, the eyes of your awareness begin to open, and the gentle whispers of your true self can speak to you over and through what begins to be recognized as the ego and the voice in your head. You begin to realize you are much more than these negative thoughts, developed patterns, past blunders, this false self. And, with this realization, you are led to the power to change these behavior patterns. *The power lies in awareness.* Your mind is no longer on autopilot; it is awake. It doesn't mean you won't have negative thoughts. You will just be aware of them. You can calm them and reason with them and overcome the behavior patterns that they drive.

Lastly, the final leg of the road to heaven through my involvement with Dress for Success Louisville, although unaware and unintentional at the time, may have been that this experience allowed me to step outside of myself and away from my fears. I turned my thoughts from complaining about how things were to the awareness of so many people and organizations that have a mission to make things better. How ironic it is that if you want to help yourself, the best medicine can be doing something for and putting your focus on another!

Service is great psychological therapy. It is proven through the success in the Alcoholics Anonymous (AA) 12-Step Program and was incorporated into the healing process. It is the last and final step and works to keep an addict on the recovery road. Step #12: "Having had a spiritual awakening as a result of these steps, we tried to carry this message to alcoholics and to practice these principles in all of our affairs." This is where they take what they have learned and share it through sponsoring and mentoring another alcoholic. This sponsorship means being available to them most anytime they may need to talk and working with them through the healing process of each of the 12 steps. They are giving back.

When my mind became trained to look for the positive, to look at a situation through the bright lens, there was another valuable lesson that came through. This lesson was that you sometimes cannot judge a situation until the big picture unfolds. You never know where you are being led. Sponsorship and counseling are a perfect example of this lesson. And the volunteers at Dress for Success Louisville who had similar experiences as the struggling women and came forth to help. In these people, they took their pain and used it for good. This gave them a wonderful opportunity to serve and to gain benefits from both ends of that service. Bill Wilson, the creator of the 12-Step Program, was an alcoholic himself. He understood from experience that service to another was an essential part of the healing process and incorporated it into the steps. This glorious feeling of euphoria from helping someone can give you a dopamine fix and a needed spiritual high that can replace the destructive high from what is referred to as "the drug of choice." This step helps the sponsor and the one being sponsored. It is an effective two-way street. It helps the sponsor, first through the feeling of service. And, secondly, it is a constant reminder for them of the 12 steps as they go through them with another. The one being sponsored is helped from knowing the sponsor has had the same experience. They appreciate they have been in their shoes and understand what they are going through, which makes them an effective counsel.

When you are doing something for another, you get out of your own head and stop focusing on your own fears and problems. It can be from a big commitment like a 12-Step sponsorship or the simple, kind gesture of being of assistance to someone by bringing them a meal or simply opening a door. The effect is the same on your heart and theirs. One may be giving, and one is receiving, but the love that is flowing is felt by both. It is a holy encounter, and it connects you to God. And where you find God, you will find heaven. And, as Dr. Dyer says, you have found it not in a place, but in the choice you made.

Seeing Love

"Become aware of what is in you,
announce it, pronounce it,
and give birth to it."

Meister Eckhart

We are all born into this world with nothing but pure love
in our hearts. Our innocent, serene, spirits first see through
rose-colored glasses, this lens that can catch and see the energy
and flow of love. It is our experiences and environment that
teach us fear. Through all my spiritual searching, the same
message kept repeating itself: there are only two emotions,
love and fear. Every positive emotion—compassion, joy,

humility, gratitude, forgiveness—all spin from love. Every negative emotion—depression, hatred, jealousy, prejudice, greed, blame, anger—the underlying emotion and source, if explored, can expose the fear. Fear is formed, programmed, and felt in the ego or mind, the false self. Love is instinctive to, created by, and experienced from the soul, your spirit, your true self. It seems the wise, elderly Cherokee Chief in the opening parable must have understood this as well. He took all those emotions that we humans battle and placed them in two categories, symbolized by a fight between two wolves.

One specific book where I read about this concept is the aforementioned book by Dr. Dan Baker, PhD., *What Happy People Know*. After making the point that there are only two emotions, love and fear, Dr. Baker goes further to explain that for those of us living in a safe environment in a first-world country, there are only two things we are afraid of: "not having enough or not being enough." Dr. Baker worked with professionally and financially successful clients struggling to find happiness. They had these things that we all believe will make us happy, and it was still elusive. Even with all their successes, these two fears could haunt them and rob them of contentment.

So, if we have only two emotions (love and fear), and we have two fears (not having enough or not being enough), this could mean we have two choices, two lenses with how to see situations and life. Do I live my life looking through the dark lens, feeding the wolf of fear? This would mean living through your ego, the voice in your head, the false self. Your complaining thoughts running rampant and no awareness of how they might be driving your actions and their destructive capacity to your spirit and those around you. This leads to condemnation of life and the world, and they are oppressive, focusing on your fears and everything that is wrong. This is a cynical perspective, and you can see no hope for change. Being negative, criticizing, and condemning situations, issues, and people comes from the ego, can feed the ego, and makes the ego feel superior. This is the ego's goal. To feel superior, to judge, and to separate.

Or do I live my life looking through a bright lens, putting my focus, thoughts and actions on solutions, hope and love? This would mean connecting with your soul, your spirit, and your true self by becoming conscious and aware of your thoughts. *Pay attention when they are going negative and not serving you or others. Then they can be interrupted and changed.* Living in a place of gratitude and focusing on goodness, hope, and abundance. You have faith in the power of the human spirit. You believe that these things surround you and are there to tap into at any time. You feel a connection rather than a separation with others. Joy resides in your heart through a place of gratitude for the wonder of life and your connections to people. I think it is impossible for the human mind to stay in this place all the time. But the more you do get there, the more you will stay there because what you focus on expands.

Here is an example of a troubling situation and the two different approaches and how it may affect the outcome. You are in a tight situation with your bills; there is not enough money to pay them; more is going out than is coming in, and you feel you are in a deep hole. Your first reaction is condemnation, which Carl Jung explains oppresses. If you look at this situation through the dark lens and condemn it, you would be thinking "There is not enough money! I cannot live on this, and I will never get out of this hole. Nothing in my life ever goes right." These thoughts create a hopeless and fearful situation. If you tell yourself, "I will never get out of this hole," you feel there is no way out. You are compulsively thinking how bad things are; your spirit is defeated, oppressed, and the wolf of fear is being fed. No solutions are being revealed because you don't believe there are any. You are not looking for solutions.

The second choice is first through acceptance. I am struggling to pay my bills; this is where I am. If you don't condemn and go toward the fear, your mind is clearer to think. This liberates you to look at the situation differently. With a different approach, there may be a solution revealed that you had not thought of before. You can look through the bright lens and focus on the positive. You are grateful you have a job and there is money coming in. In this state of gratitude, you begin to put focus on and realize what you do have and what is really important: your family, your friends, and your health. Gratitude unlocks your mind, and positive thoughts can begin to flow. You quiet your ego by becoming aware of negative thoughts as they surface. You replace and overpower them with grateful thoughts for what you have and prayer for direction and answers. You put your ego aside and are accountable for your role in the situation. Maybe I'm not the best at handling money and could use some help. You realize a financial literacy class could be a benefit to help you better manage your money. You believe there is help and support out there if you look. You take action and sign up for a class and learn a better way to budget what you have coming in. In this, you see the benefit of how this financial literacy class will add skills to your life and make you more capable. You put your focus on and appreciate what you have, and through this exercise you may realize there are things you really don't need. You affirm that yes, you have made some mistakes, but you didn't know better. This situation sent you looking for lessons that have taught you to be better. What a blessing!! You can believe that there was love in the situation. This love was guiding you to learn, to become stronger and more capable. You became empowered and more confident through this journey.

Looking through the dark lens or the bright lens, feeding the wolf of fear or the wolf of love, living through your false self or your true self or living through your ego or your soul—all of these are metaphors for choices of how to live. This is an extreme challenge and genuine feat for the human brain to overcome. Dr. Dan O'Grady, a psychologist and one of the Center for Action and Contemplation's Living School students, says in one of Father Richard Rohr's daily meditations that "our negative thoughts are like Velcro; they stick and hold: whereas our positive thoughts are like Teflon, they slide away." We must deliberately choose to hold onto positive thoughts. He goes on to say that "neuroscience can now demonstrate that the brain indeed has a negative bias; the brain prefers to constellate around fearful, negative, or problematic situations." This explains our draw to drama, violent and scary movies, fear driven politics, and negative media.

I had an experience through my involvement with Dress for Success Louisville that confirms this. Our organization learned there was a grant available through the government program HUD (Housing and Urban Development) that we wanted to apply for. Our non-profit was newly formed, completely volunteer driven, and we did not have a lot of experience. Here is an example of the goodness that was revealed to me through my involvement. Our local Housing Authority was applying for the grant as well and had experience. They willingly offered their time, expertise, and assistance to introduce us to this very complicated process. They offered to meet with me on a Monday morning. I showed up, and we first had introductions and small talk. In this conversation, they were still excited from their weekend. Several residents

had successfully completed the program they offer to gain
employment and financial independence and were moving out
of the government housing. They had graduated out of this
program. They mark this accomplishment with a ceremony
and celebration. I was in awe of the number in the program
that had moved on to self-sufficiency and was soaking up their
excitement. This was hope and success! I said to them, "You
guys should have called the news stations to report on this."
They told me they call them every year when the graduation
is held, but they rarely show up.

With all this newly found goodness and hope, I decided to
write a letter to all of our four local news stations. I suggested
that maybe the paradigm was shifting, and they could report
more of these positive stories that I was witnessing. I thought
maybe they hadn't thought of this angle and that people
wanted to hear more of these. I was naive to this scientific
knowledge from Dr. Dan O'Grady at the time, that the human
brain is biased toward negativity. But my response from the
news stations confirmed this. I never heard from three of them
and appreciated the general manager of one of them taking
the time to write me back and respond. He told me they have

done surveys and studies and that positive stories are not what people want to hear. They sprinkle them in and sometimes end the news cast on a positive note. But mostly, people want to know what they need to be afraid of. This genetic bias leads us to feed the fear, which allows that fear to fester. Then the fear expands, and we all feel the effects of this fear. It is spread across the air waves, the internet, and through conversations. We can become like Mark Twain, having a lot of worries in our life, most of which never happened. We have spent precious, limited time in fear and missed time that could be spent in heaven.

This is how we are controlled. A lot of institutions figured out they could control people through fear. It will get and hold their attention. And it appeals to our egos. The ego is where this negative bias we are prone to resides. We become more and more divisive because we listen to what appeals to our egos, the side we are on. We believe we are right, and the other side is wrong. This makes the ego feel superior and feeds it. This can come through in politics, social issues, or religions for example. The ego wants to separate us into sides; the soul wants connection. The negativity thrown at each of the other sides expands and grows because with so much negative focus the effect is negative expansion. In politics, each side spends so much negative energy condemning the other side and spreading fear. This is proof that "condemnation does not liberate; it oppresses." This condemnation keeps expanding and growing and results in gridlock.

News is information about events that affect our lives. Because of humanity's negative bias, we have come to see news as the events that negatively affect our lives. Things we need to be afraid of. We can blame the messengers, but they are giving us what we respond to. I began to tell myself "This is news!" when I would witness positive events and successes. This is affecting people's lives but in a positive way! I witnessed so much "good news" that you don't see reported. I found that there is so much more good news and acts of kindness and compassion. You just would never know it by only paying attention to the reported news. By focusing on this, I used the bright lens to change my perspective about news. I created my own news station in my mind seeing and confirming the abundance of goodness in the world. The more I observed, the more things seemed to appear. What I was focused on showed up and grew! This changed my perspective about what is possible and my perspective about the world.

How do we balance being aware and cautious or going down a rabbit hole of fear? How do we flip that lens from darkness to light? Dr. Dan Baker, PhD., states that it is impossible to feel fear and gratitude at the same time. Intentionally changing your lens to gratitude allows you to savor your positive thoughts and keep your focus on blessings and hope, which in turn overpowers, diminishes, and allows you to starve that wolf of fear. When I would hear about fearful, troubling actions, I would turn my focus to the victorious programs and stories in my awareness that were working to change and lift lives. *To the solutions.* Rather than feeling hopeless, this allowed me to see hope. I was so grateful I had been exposed to these organizations so I could find hope.

Could we possibly be at a turning point in our human evolution that we became aware of that genetic bias and collectively work to overcome, rise above, and create a more harmonious world? Could we be shifting the paradigm to craving our connections and spreading "good news"? Imagine the possibilities of more of the solutions and good news spreading over the air waves, across the internet, and through conversations. When I look through the bright lens, I feel that if people are aware of this genetic bias and can realize this, maybe we will become better. Until the mind begins to awaken to this truth, it lives through the ego on autopilot, and it criticizes and dominates. Through being awake and aware, more of our actions and thoughts could come from our connectedness and compassion. What you focus on expands and works collectively as well as individually. I can see love working toward fulfilling this awakening. This brings me the hope and the ability to have faith and pray that we reach for and accomplish this paradigm shift—a mass shrinking of egos and separateness to realize the expansion of our connected souls.

We naturally and understandably come to know fear through our pain and suffering. This very suffering, if transformed, is fulfilling its purpose to awaken us. This is why so many people don't change their negative patterns until they hit rock bottom. The deep suffering is the jolt they need to live their life differently. Father Rohr says, "If we don't transform our pain, we most assuredly will transmit it." Our world is challenged by people guilty of nothing more than seeing through a dark lens and transmitting their fears and pain. The pain builds up like a volcano waiting to erupt! If it doesn't fulfill this purpose of transformation and drawing you closer to God, it begins to boil. The weary mind, exhausted body, and wounded spirit can only hold down and suppress the pain for so long, and then it must explode and be transmitted. Some will transmit on themselves, and some will transmit on others—or both. This is also something to keep in mind when someone's pain erupts on you. Knowing this, you realize that you don't have to take it personally and not to be insulted. It may have absolutely nothing to do with you. You are the scape goat for their pain. This could also bring you to a place of compassion that could be grace for them.

With each wound that we carry and every pain that we experience, we have a choice of how we will react to it. We can react from a place of fear, holding onto the heavy burden, allowing it to bring bitterness and harden our heart. Or we can react from a place of love, allowing it to teach us the intended lesson, connecting us deeper to our spirit, awakening and transforming us. Bitterness, depression, and fear are a dense, unbreakable wall that stops the flow of love. While this quote has been attributed to Buddha, Haruki Murakami, and the Dalai Lama, the meaning is what's important. "Pain is inevitable, suffering is optional." Living in the darkness of the past experience and not making use of the pain for "pruning," change, and transformation can be what is creating suffering. Again, condemning the pain oppresses you. Feeling anger, which is deep down fear in disguise, creates suffering. If allowed, the pain can be a teacher.

The egoic mind wants to cling to the pain, victimize it, and identify with it. It wants to hang onto it and create more suffering. Or there may be another destructive path trying to numb it and avoid it, which allows it to fester and grow, the effects of which cause more pain. Staring down the pain through a new lens is the tool you need to utilize in order to find the transformative power the pain can hold, to see what could be learned and how it can change you. This practice can bring you to the "secrets of your heart" that love is trying to expose to you. The bright lens looks for the love, the lesson, and the awakening in your suffering to transform it so you do not transmit it on yourself or others. The lesson is always to find love, forgiveness, humility, compassion, connection, and strength through God. Putting on this bright lens provides a tool to practice or work out our brain, to overcome our human tendency toward negativity, accomplish being grateful, and awaken the soul to the heaven and love within. It can remind you that God is in the pain and God is in the joy. God's love can be seen everywhere and in all of it. And this bright lens can make you aware of the light and love that resides in you so that you may "announce it, pronounce it, and give birth to it" so that you may give birth to your true self.

The Hope

"You may say I'm a dreamer, but I'm not
the only one. I hope someday you'll join
us. And the world can live as one."

John Lennon and Yoko Ono

There is hope found in dreams, and it is boundless. Hope is the
motivator for the dream. Without the hope, there is no dream,
and without the dream, there is no hope. The ancient Greek
word for hope is *elpo*. The meaning of *elpo* is to anticipate or
welcome the expectation of that which is certain. Maybe hope
is not something that we search for but a glorious feeling we
naturally anticipate by having unshakeable faith and all of its

grace. There are no restrictions or limits on this anticipation, and it is open to all who feel the calling. When John Lennon and Yoko Ono penned the lyrics to the song "Imagine" all those years ago, I have to believe they were calling us all to join in the dream that would give us hope. Results may not always be what we hoped for and when we needed them, but if you can feel the presence of God and love in any situation or person, the soul feels fulfilled and experiences the expectation of what is certain. That certainty is that God is there. The hope is found and achieved through the power of God's love. And therein lies the hope.

No one knows this better than Father Gregory Boyle, author and founder of Homeboy Industries in Los Angeles, the largest gang rehabilitation and re-entry program in the world. For gang members, the fear that lives in the mind is ever present and created by the ominous outer reality of violence, danger, and poverty—a life that is all they have ever known and ambushes their very being. Many would say they live in a hopeless world.

Father Boyle, or "G" as he is lovingly referred to by the "homies," is quoted as saying, "We seek a compassion that stands in awe of the pain that some people must carry rather than in judgment of how they carry it." When we can recognize that this is a suffering human who is transmitting his erupting pain, we can see them through a whole different lens. We are able to validate their dignity, connect soul to soul, and send compassion to a vibrational level that lifts up this expansive yearning universe. We can "stand with them" as Father Boyle says, hold them in our hearts, and understand that their pain runs so deep that they have been blinded from knowing or seeing any love. We begin to understand that change can only happen when something or someone breaks their heart open and allows powerful grace to trickle in.

Author and international advocate for children Peter Mutabazi ran away from home and an abusive father at age ten and survived for five years on the streets of Kampala, Uganda, a city of 1.5 million. He encountered the kindness of a complete stranger, who saw his humanity and potential. This stranger paid to send Peter to a boarding school, which resulted in changing and altering his life path. Since this experience, Peter has gone on to foster many children and adopt several as his own. In Peter's book *Now I am Known*, he speaks of the greatest gift this school gave him: patience. He writes:

"They didn't expect me to come off the city streets and suddenly act like everyone else. They let me be me and move at my own pace. One of the greatest myths I run into today is that if we change someone's circumstances, we will automatically change their life. The idea is easy to believe if you haven't come from a hard place. The truth is trauma's impact lasts much longer than the trauma itself. It shapes you and impacts how you see and interact with the world. Simply removing someone from their source of trauma does not heal the mind, soul, or spirit."

These traumas and the defense and reactions to the traumas become programmed in the brain, in the ego. Peter's experience shows that patience is an extreme act of love and a grace that can give a soul hope and heal a wounded heart.

What gives hope to those that live in a hopeless world consumed with the cycle of violence, poverty, and fear? It's hard for me to imagine how someone who has suffered trauma, abuse, and neglect can see through that affliction. Their eyes know no difference, have no ability to visualize a dream, and can't even perceive hope. If they were never shown love, they would not have an understanding or a concept of love. Maybe the life-changing purpose of the bright lens for them is on the receiving end. It becomes a lens to show and express this unknown emotion, love, to them. Those of us foreign to this kind of hopelessness can change our eyewear and gaze at them with loving patience, non-judgmental eyes, and send them the message that "they are known," we see their worth, and we recognize that they have unbearable pain. This pain has nowhere to go but to be transmitted to others unless it is met with patience and love. This is the life-changing work of Homeboy Industries. The compassion and love shown to the homies, penetrates the darkness of their spirit and ignites a spark that brings forth the love and the potential that has been handcuffed with pain. You can be an empathetic presence for a wounded soul. That is an enormous power and generosity we hold through a simple, compassionate gaze. With that gaze and understanding, we can make another soul feel worthy, which may grant them hope.

There is so much to learn from pain. We can learn from

our own pain, and we can learn from the pain of others. I have
had the privilege and honor of being invited to and observing Alcoholics Anonymous meetings. At the meetings, I have
heard addiction referred to as a spiritual wound, a separation
from your God or, as they refer to him, your Higher Power.
These meetings are quietly being held all around, at all hours
of the day, and available to anyone who is in need. They are
meetings that offer hope. The meetings I attended have been
a spiritual experience where the presence of a God or a Higher
Power fills the room. "Blessed are the poor in spirit, for theirs
is the Kingdom of Heaven" (Matthew 5:3). I felt this heaven
that they possess. Their souls become one, sacredly connected
in their shared suffering, pain, vulnerability, and humility.
And they are connected by the faith, hope, and strength they
find through their Higher Power. They bear their souls, and
no one can judge because they have all been there. The ego or
false self is left at the door. The first step is about losing your
ego. "We admit we are powerless over alcohol, and our lives
have become unmanageable." Step 2: "Came to believe that a
power greater than ourselves could restore us to sanity." That
pain and that power connect them at the soul level, and it's a

brotherhood / sisterhood like no other. It is also a proven path that, when followed, leads to healing and sanity.

Those in the program that reach true healing, wholeness, and recovery are the happiest, most joyful people I have encountered. They are a high voltage light for the world. They have used their wounds and pain to gain wisdom and to transform their lives and their spirits.

Life is yin and yang. Without darkness, could we know light? Without experiencing pain, could we understand and feel intense joy? Once healed, maybe they can feel this illuminating joy deeper because they have been through excruciating suffering. They learn to take one step at a time, one moment at a time, and live in the present because rebuilding your entire life is too overwhelming when you look too far into the future. Their lives have been shattered by choices driven by their disease and must be rebuilt from the ground up with mountains to climb. Their brokenness dismantled their families, created enormous debt, lost jobs, and isolated and ravaged their spirits. Their lives became whole again through humility, gratitude, and the service they do in sponsoring another who is where they have been. The 12-Step Program is inner hard work, and each participant commits to doing the soul searching and digging that leads them to an awakening and the wisdom that brings them to the Kingdom of Heaven. It is in this they find and stay connected to their Higher Power and find this joy that now lives in their hearts.

I learned so much of what is possible by observing and listening during these AA meetings. So much can be taught to us by connecting to others' pain. We can learn humility by observing them surrender. We can learn courage and strength by observing how they persevere. We can learn faith and hope through their determination and commitment. We can learn acceptance by observing how they manage their difficult path. We can be inspired to be better by watching them become better through such challenging struggles. We can use these lessons as grace and the spiritual energy for us to grow closer to this Power that, if connected to and found, can restore sanity, and turn a life around. We can learn that forgiveness is possible by observing how they are able to forgive themselves for wrong to others and forgive others who have wronged them. When you witness forgiveness, you see a spirit lift and a life change by mastering this ultimate act of love. We learn compassion by "standing in awe of the pain some people must carry." Through their pain we can find and learn hope.

In his best-selling book *Tattoos on the Heart*, Father Boyle tells us that "it is an essential tenet of Buddhism that we begin to change the world by first changing how we look at the world." We can change our lens to put more focus on this abundance of goodness, love, and hope that is already there, and this can bring us to find and see our connection. This connection can bring us to this place where "the world can live as one." That is the hope and harmonious dream that John Lennon chanted and planted in our souls. We apply this dream for the world, motivated by our hope for the world and bring to focus the love that is flowing so freely. The world becomes a divine magnet, producing, creating, and experiencing more of what we see and think. Just imagine …

Becoming Grace

"How wonderful it is that nobody need wait a single moment before starting to improve the world."

Anne Frank

Author Gary Zukav, in the best-selling book *Seat of the Soul*, defines grace as "spiritual energy." Grace is a gift, a gift that is gratefully received and intentionally given. It can come to us through acts of kindness, generosity, and compassion. But it also approaches us disguised through challenges and pain. This is sometimes hard to perceive as grace. It may take the bright lens to recognize this energy that is being given to your spirit when it comes in this way. Life may be trying to teach you and lead you to the "secrets of your heart." Anytime growth and wisdom are achieved, you have turned this spiritual energy that life has sent to you into grace.

Grace is delivered through the enormous power of love and can come from earthly angels. If you are awake and aware enough, you will notice it being delivered from heavenly angels. It is sometimes an invisible act and sometimes an obvious act. When we look through the bright lens, we can recognize and capture this abundance of grace that surrounds us. We are in tune to the friendly actions of everyday people and witness their kindness. The eyes that have been altered by this lens are also aware of the two-way street offered from grace. These bright eyes create a path for your spirit to see and receive grace. And they are a vessel for circling back and sending grace back into the world. It takes very little to make a profound difference in someone's life. Sometimes it's so easily done that you may not even realize you've done anything at all. But, even without that realization about their life, you have certainly made a difference in your own life. You have poured out love and improved the world. Grace is a loving, flowing energy. When we channel it, we are giving the world a gift.

A state of gratitude will also lift and fill your mind and heart with this spiritual energy. An intentional, conscious shift in focus from thankless to grateful will create an inner seismic shift that will flow through every core of your being. Author Sarah Ban Breathnach's book, *Simple Abundance*, offers a path to achieve a life filled with simplicity, order, harmony, beauty, and joy. Sarah tells us, "These principles will not blossom and flourish without gratitude." Why? She says it is "because you simply will not be the same person two months from now after consciously giving thanks each day for the abundance that exists in your life. And you will have set in motion an ancient spiritual law; the more you have and are grateful for, the more will be given to you."

I became so grateful for this grace that brought me to see life in this way and know that this grace and energy are contagious! We all have the capacity and power within us to create a brighter reality by simply changing our thoughts. We can awaken each day and center your thoughts on what you are grateful for and what is good. Usher in your day calling to mind, or maybe writing down, a quick inventory of your blessings. This begins your day on the right foot, lifts your soul, and sets your attitude and mood. Through this choice you are enhancing your life, lifting those around you, and making the world a better place. The greater good is served by bringing brightness and a smile to the world.

Author and spiritual teacher, Eckhart Tolle, in his best-selling book *A New Earth*, enlightens us with his wisdom on the ego and thoughts. He tells us, "To end the misery that has afflicted the human condition for thousands of years, you have to start with yourself and take responsibility for your inner state at any given moment." He says to ask yourself, "Is there negativity in me at this moment?" Then become alert, attentive to your thoughts as well as your emotions. He goes on to say, "The moment you become aware of a negative state within yourself, it does not mean you have failed, it means you have succeeded." Again, this awareness of your thoughts is the beginning of being conscious, awakened, saved, and changing your life. This is your soul, aware of your ego, your essence and truest self, aware of your false self. To give more perspective, he explains: "Negativity is a disease on our planet. What pollution is on the outer level is negativity on the inner." Our pessimistic, complaining thoughts, words, and actions pollute our own spirits and the spirits of those who allow themselves to take them in. And these thoughts, words, and actions do absolutely nothing to lift and improve our world.

Our thoughts create our energy. We have all experienced it. A person or family member "lights up a room." Or a person or family member enters a room and the "tension could be cut with a knife." The energy they bring is carried by their manner and demeanor, which is an effect of their thoughts. What else could it be if the feeling in the room can be changed just by their entrance? The hard stiffness and negative thoughts or the gentle grace that you carry is felt and absorbed by those you encounter. This is another enormous power we each hold. With each thought, word, and action that vibrates and flows from love, we are building up, advancing, and making the world a better place.

We are all here on this earth trying to make our way. For some, the circumstances and experiences are traumatic, excruciating, and much more challenging than for others. No matter our background, we all come here without defined instructions to maneuver our way through life, so we learn as we go. If we see through this lens, it puts us all in the same boat. We are all souls on a journey. We are all flawed humans with goodness and God in our souls. This equalizes us and gives us a sacred connection. This is a connection that should also give us understanding. By recognizing this, you can be compassionate grace to someone whose journey is difficult, and they are dancing with a realization. Your understanding, kindness, and grace could be the dance partner that leads them and opens their eyes to the awakening and connection their soul is searching for. Your showing them love and patience could allow them to find the love and patience in themselves. Again, the effect is the same on your heart and theirs because when you make a difference in someone's journey, it also affects yours in return. You have allowed love to flow. You have channeled grace to make someone's life better, and this has a profound effect on the whole of "life's heart."

On the last day of the year in Sarah's *Simple Abundance* book of daily meditations, when the transformative annual journey is completed, we are told the new journey begins. Sarah tells us: "No longer will you see things as they are. You will see things as you are." When you live and see through the bright lens, you are a light that guides and shines, a positive flowing force and divine grace to the world. You are a giver and, because everything is returned to you, a joyous receiver. And you have not waited "a single moment before starting to improve the world."

Experiencing The Miracle

"There are only two ways to live your life.
One is as though nothing is a miracle. The
other is as though everything is a miracle."

Albert Einstein

My journey took me from living through a cynical, fearful
mind to finding and living from my hopeful, joyful soul. This
resulted in a miraculous shift that changed my course. We all
live in the same world, but the world is not the same for any
of us. There are over 8 billion people living on this earth. That

would present over 8 billion views of the world we live in. This is because we all bring our experiences and emotions, our lens, to form our perceptions. Added to that is each person's different and unique DNA that determines and filters how we handle and process those emotions. Since we all have different experiences, emotions, and DNA, this gives us all different perceptions. I have heard of two different people living in the same neighborhood; one would say it is a friendly neighborhood, and the other would say it is an unfriendly neighborhood. It's like a self-fulfilled prophecy. What you believe and what you give out is what you will see and receive. I also find it so interesting when siblings, reflecting on family situations, can remember the situation so differently. They are looking through the lens that their emotions and experiences bring to form their perception of the situation. How gracious that life gives us the freedom to choose our own perceptions, to form our own lens. I think this is what Sarah Ban Breathnach is referring to when she states: "No longer will you see things as they are, you will see things as you are." The inner work, exploration, and journey that you take through her daily meditation book will change your lens and how you view and approach life.

What was miraculous about my transformation? Nothing changed outwardly. There was no lightning bolt or plume of smoke that appeared and left behind a Camelot or Utopia. The world was still the exact same. But, for me it seemed and felt like a completely different world. Looking at the world and my life through this bright lens that I chose brought to focus all the goodness, blessings, and hope that was always there. It was all around me waiting to be found and seen. When I focused on it, it kept expanding and growing.

A Course in Miracles was published in 1976 and written by Helen Schucman. It is considered a collection of guiding principles to healing and wholeness. This continuing theme I incurred through my spiritual searching, that there is only fear and love, is a primary principle of the course. The course teaches that the shift in perception that creates the miracle is the shift from fear to love because that is all there is. The course also teaches that fear is darkness, the absence of love, and error. Similarly, the origin of the word sin in both Hebrew and Greek means "to miss the mark or goal." Jesus tells us the greatest commandment is to love one another as I have loved you. This must be the mark that we reach for, the goal. Error, fear, and sin can only live and be created at the ego level, in the mind.

And the course teaches that love is joy and God and light. The soul level is where joy is found, and God and light live and arise. When we act or react from a negative place—a place of fear—we error, we sin, we "miss the mark." There is no error at the level of our soul, only perfection, and we all hold this perfection. We are all wonderfully created children of God. When we take our pain that we are so afraid of and transform it by looking for the love in the pain, we can move away from fear and trust that God is there. This is our purpose: to experience a transformation of the mind, which creates the realization of our perfect, connected souls. The realization that God is in us. This is the awakening, rebirth, salvation, and consciousness. All the world's wisdom traditions teach and describe an experience of realization, just in different ways.

The phrase "Do not be afraid" is stated in the Bible 365 times. You could say, one reminder for each day of the year. Fr. Richard Rohr tells us in another of his daily meditations that "the Greek word for 'repent' (metanoia) means to change your mind." When we are called to repent, we are called to a shift or change of mind. The mind is where our experiences, emotions, and DNA come together to form our perceptions and where fear and ego resides. Metanoia calls us to change our way of thinking, a new way of living and a new way of seeing.

But wait!! What?!! We need to change this survival instinct that dominates our DNA? This instinct to assess, judge, criticize and be afraid? Our egos are formed from birth and grow with us! You want us to dismiss this sense that has lead and dominated beings and interests for centuries?! This would take a miracle! I guess that is why it can be perceived as such. And, I guess knowing that to thrive as a species, "change your mind" would speak to tell this story. This story that we need to shift and evolve from mind, ego-dominated humans to find our soul and our connection.

It is no wonder that with humanity's negative bias, we took these words—sin and repent—and attached them to an adverse meaning and definition. Man could not see the "good news" that was being offered. Simply change your mind and keep this changed mind on the mark. Our wise and loving God who created us, was fully aware of our stubborn egos, our negative bias, and our resistance to change. Maybe that is why "Do not be afraid" needed to be stated 365 times.

This doesn't mean fear is always bad or we won't experience

fear. It would be impossible to be human and not experience fear. Sometimes the fear is trying to teach us, wake us up, send us a needed message. In Sarah Ban Breathnach's *Simple Abundance* book, Sarah tells us "to take comfort in remembering that courage is fear that has said her prayers." Our fear calls us to talk to God, turn it over to God, and then be patient and pay attention. Be awake and aware so you can recognize the promptings of spirit that arrive wrapped in loving grace. When you unwrap this gift of grace, there you will find the hope and faith that God will guide and direct you. You have shifted from the fear, the error, the sin, and put your focus on the enormous power of God's love. You have experienced a miracle.

Once the miracle has occurred and you have experienced the joy and the bliss, there is no going back. There may be peaks and valleys, but the mind can never forget the way life can be when lived through love and the eyes of your soul. You are conscious, awake, saved, and unified with the source, nature, and all of humanity! There is no more division, only this awakening and awareness of a presence, which is infinite pure love, God, and amazing grace.

When Jesus was on the cross, moments before he left this

earth, he said, "Father forgive them, they know not what they do." (Luke 23:34) I have come to see these words as the most important words that Jesus spoke: that is unconditional love. His compassion and asking for their forgiveness in the face of his suffering said that he understood they were not awake. He understood they had not shifted their minds. Jesus was disrupting the status quo. The established order of social status and power by the collective mindset, the collective ego, was being thrown into disorder by this new lens that Jesus offered. He said "see" these people. Recognize their humanity and divinity. The beggars, the prostitutes, the tax collectors, the lepers, that had been dismissed, discarded, and out of their sight, he was bringing to focus. He was showing the lowly compassion and understanding when the natural order was to ignore them. He was telling them that these people were important, worthy, and sacred. This stripped his opponents of their ego comparison that they were better and more important than them. Their ego's felt threatened and kicked into survival mode. Their instinct and response was fear.

This prompted the collective wolf of fear to become very hungry and needy because change is scary and challenging for the ego. To fight the change, the fear kept spreading, and the crowds became a feeding ground for the wolf of fear. Jesus was offering them a radical new lens and a new authority. An authority based on love, not the social order and ego power, which was all they had known. This was foreign to them, and they were not ready to accept it. Jesus understood this. In his crucifixion, he completely starved his wolf of fear. His lens that viewed all people as sacred, never dimmed, shaded, or hued dark.

God has been patiently waiting for 2,000+ years for our eyes to be open to the potential of a change of mind. Patiently waiting for us to be ready and embrace a new perspective. Patiently waiting for a shift to a new way of thinking, away from our egos, toxicity, and fear. I think this loving God that created us, being fully aware of the fear built into our DNA, understood it would take centuries of evolution and better understanding to conquer this bias. Centuries to transform our collective hearts, accept this "good news," and awaken to this truth. He has been sending us mystics and teachers throughout the centuries to plant the seeds. The roots are stabilizing, and the seeds are bearing fruit. This fruit is wonderful bounty for the wolf of love. When I look through the bright lens, I can see God at work and the fruit cultivating, ripening, and growing. I think he wonders ... are they ready now? We understood that Jesus could perform miracles. Are we ready to collectively grasp and believe that we can?

How can we carry out this shift we are being asked to perform? The Buddhist say "to change the world, you must first change the way you 'look' at the world." Sarah Ban Breathnach tells us "no longer will you see things as they are; you will 'see' things as you are." It would appear that our eyes hold the key. This shift is carried out by accepting a radical new lens. Instead of fear, see love, and then you will be love. Instead of despair, find and see hope, and then you will be hope. Instead of judgement and criticism, find and see the good, and then you will be the good. Instead of darkness, see light, and you will become light.

I have tremendous hope and can feel God in the energy and rising of a mass awakening that has been evolving for centuries. The turmoil, rebellion, confusion, and turbulence we are experiencing are the labor pains for the birth of this miracle. Nothing in nature is born without pain, and fear is fighting back and holding on. The collective wolf of fear is loud, hungry, and demanding food. The wolf of love is whispering, waiting, and ever so grateful for each bite of flourishing fruit. Pure, true love doesn't need to fight. "The best criticism of the bad is the practice of the good." Jesus revealed this. This pure, true love, just is; it is a light and compass to joy and the peace that passes all understanding.

Symbols can drive actions. Whether the symbol of the bright lens came from the wolf of love or through the power of the Holy Spirit, I just know love was behind it. I know for sure because its purpose was to bring her to focus. In sharing it, my hope is that this symbol can drive actions toward metanoia. Stir emotions to shift our minds and change our ego thinking away from criticism, condemnation, negativity, fear, and toxicity so we can begin to understand what we can create when we do. So that we can understand the good news that would flourish. That would be a collectively created miracle that would allow all of us to live our lives, as Albert Einstein says, in such a way that you can see "everything as a miracle."

The Lens To Hope And Joy

"Some things cannot be taught, but they can be awakened in the heart. Spirituality is recognizing the divine light that is within us all. It doesn't belong to any particular religion; it belongs to everyone."

Muhammed Ali

Dr. Lisa Miller, PhD, is a researcher, psychologist, and author of *The Awakened Brain: The New Science of Spirituality and Our Quest for an Inspired Life*. She began to notice that spirituality had a strong, positive impact on her patients, their depression and issues. Curious, she launched into research to understand this phenomenon. In her book, the findings of this research and breakthrough scientific discovery of spirituality's effects on the brain revealed: "The awakened brain is the neural circuitry that allows us to see the world more fully and thus enhance our individual, societal, and global well-being." She goes on to say, "When we awaken, we feel more fulfilled and at home in the world, and we build relationships and make decisions from a wider view. We move from loneliness and isolation to connection; from competition and division to compassion and altruism; from an entrenched focus on our wounds, problems, and losses to a fascination with the journey of life." These findings confirm that an awakening in the soul, physically and scientifically, impacts and carries over into your brain and it will enhance every aspect of your life. Your being awake and aware of your thoughts and your spirit, also enhances your community and the world.

Was the explanation for the effects of my new bright lens really just giving me eyes that were seeing through the awareness of my awakened soul and mind? I believe it was. Once I became awake, the lens was a valuable symbol and constant reminder to stay awake and keep me on course. I found the symbol is much needed because the wolf of fear, the ego, doesn't go away just because you are awake. It is always fighting to regain control, to creep back in, keep fear alive, and stop the flow of love and gratitude. This false self wants to deny you joy.

In trying to define the big feeling from this little word, joy, two words that kept popping up were deep and intense. Happiness, although a much bigger word, is short in shelf life, fleeting, comes and goes. Joy settles in and makes itself at home.

What is an awakening? As Muhammed Ali reminds us, if it can't be taught, how do you attain it? The first, and very important, step is again, being aware and conscious of your thoughts. Author Marianne Williamson is quoted as saying "Thought is cause; experience is effect." More often than not, it is this effect of an experience that prompts the awakening. When you come to the realization that your thoughts could be the cause of some of your misery, like I did early in the story, this awareness can prompt and guide you to recognize those thoughts. Or it could be prompted by an event that rocks you to your core and sends you to your knees with nowhere else to go. You begin to look for answers and comfort and hope. So it is an opportunity that arises that must be seized.

Whatever the cause that brings you to the awareness of

your thoughts, you are then recognizing there are these two parts: your ego and your soul, or your false self and your true self, the wolf of fear or the wolf of love. The ego is on the surface, your incessant thoughts, focused on lack—never enough, never good enough. This is where your developed negative patterns and fears come through. Your soul, your true self, lies deep within, waiting to be recognized and brought forth. Your soul holds your compassion, patience, and love. When it is more important to be love than to be right, you can recognize that the ego is shrinking. Once you become aware of your thoughts, the second step is exploration to get through the ego and discover your soul, your light within. You are literally "soul searching," trying to get through the ego to find this soul where unconditional and pure love resides.

Meister Eckhart was a German Catholic theologian, philosopher, and mystic who died in 1328. He wrote: "There is a journey you must take. It is a journey without destination. There is no map. Your soul will lead you. And you can take nothing with you." This journey is traveled by spending time in quiet, contemplative thought, reading, and meditation; an inner journey. It will be time well spent that leads

you to a treasure, a treasure that can only be found by traveling within. It may be the most important and the only journey you ever take where there is no outer movement. You
must travel through the ego to truly find your soul. It can be
difficult, hard work, like labor, giving birth to your true self.
When you can recognize your egoic thoughts and fears and
can understand and examine how they became developed
patterns, then you have been led to your soul. Once found,
you can understand and make peace with your fears, and the
power is there to change your thoughts and the behaviors they
drive. When Meister Eckhart says "take nothing with you," I
believe he is saying leave all you think you know, your ego. Be
humble so you can be open to this new knowledge that will
reveal itself. This knowledge that you are the love found in
your heart. And that you are "a fragment of life's heart." This
knowledge that you have the power to change your thoughts
and change the effects of those thoughts. An awakening also
uncovers a connection and feels this connection to everything
and all that is. An awakened soul recognizes the divine light
that is within us all.

If joy is a "deep" feeling, my sense tells me that it is found in and comes from a deep place. Joy is found when you have awakened, when you have found your soul. That joy settles in, makes itself at home, and comes through as you live from your true self. You act and react from a place of love.

A soul who has experienced an awakening, besides being conscious of their thoughts, has eyes that see and a sense that is aware of divine synchronicities. These synchronicities are coincidences that cannot be explained, angels at work. For example, you make a wrong turn and then run into someone you haven't seen for a long time, and you help them, or they help you in a situation. Or you meet someone new that gives you an idea you hadn't thought of before that helps you through a challenge. Another example, a good Samaritan shows up exactly when you need them during a trying circumstance. Carl Jung, the great Swiss psychiatrist believed that such "meaningful coincidences" play an important role in our life. Albert Einstein stated that "a coincidence is God's way of remaining anonymous." This organizing energy force is another form of incredible grace that, when recognized, can be used as a holy compass. These synchronicities can be your confirmation that God is with you, holding your hand and leading the way. This fills you with faith and hope, that certainty again from the word hope, that God is there.

How can the symbol of the bright lens assist you in achieving this deep, intense feeling of joy? How can the lens assist you in achieving the awakening that brings joy with it? How can it bring you to see hope? It can be a practical and useful tool to trigger, remind, and direct your thoughts.

Make use of the lens to bring you to a place of stillness. It can prompt you to be present. We spend so much time "in our heads" and very little time observing our surroundings and being present. The glasses can prompt you to look around and be aware of what is in front of and what is around you. Recognize with your full attention the brilliant colors, singing birds, and beauty in nature when you step outside. Recognize with your full attention the delicious food in front of you and savor each bite you take. Recognize with your full attention the person sitting in front of you and fully listen to the words you exchange. Listen to the melody of a song and feel how it lifts your spirits. While taking a walk, expand your vision, pay attention to the path, and see the wonder of creation. God is always found in the gift of the present moment. Where you see

God, there can be joy. How astonishing that in a split second we can reach this joy simply by becoming present and shifting our awareness.

The lens can be used to help you recognize and identify the wolf of fear, your ego. It can serve to trigger and interrupt programmed, destructive thoughts. This can help you "see" when you are coming from your false self and help you redirect your thoughts to a positive source, a source for good, a source of love. It can benefit you to hold the feeling in your heart in an awakened state.

The symbol of the bright lens is useful to guide your perception. It can spark a reminder not to judge a situation until the big picture unfolds and to look for the transformative power and growth in a circumstance. Use it to see that this circumstance could be leading you somewhere you hadn't thought of. For instance, I hear so often of people being devastated at the loss of a job only to take their career in a completely different direction and feel this new place is where they were meant to be, not realizing when it happened that it was a blessing.

It can offer assistance in seeing a person differently. To call to mind patience, understanding, and to look for the good in people, not to judge because you don't know what that person's pain has been or what their circumstances are. We are naturally drawn toward light. The bright lens can lead you to a glimpse of the light that radiates and glows within everyone, even when their light has been dimmed from trauma and painful conditions. When there is a swelling of compassion from your heart, it serves to speak with your eyes and say, I "see" you, your humanity, and your pain.

When your mood is down, the shift this lens can provide can brighten your day. It can help to trigger thoughts of gratitude and put focus on the abundance of blessings in your life when you are having a hard time seeing them. Once you begin to make a mental list and bring into your awareness these things to be grateful for, you can go down a rabbit hole and completely turn your mood and your day around. For instance, bring to front of mind, I have food on our table, a roof over our head, a bed to sleep in, clothes to wear, and a family to love. You can go on and on and challenge your perception from troubles and lack to find blessings and abundance.

Use the bright lens to advance you toward metanoia, a

change of mind that will lead to a change in your heart. Let it prompt a reminder when you are feeling pessimism, condemnation, negative thinking and mind pollution. Allow it to guide you to change how you look at the world so you can change the world. This change of mind brings along with it boundless hope.

I have always loved the song "What a Wonderful World," sung by Louis Armstrong. When I hear this song, I feel a soaring in my heart and a singing in my soul. I can feel the optimism and love coming from deep within his spirit. His words and melody make known the powerful connection between the earth, the simple things in life, and the joy found when you are aware and grateful for both. I believe this song is expressing this connection when he is singing:

"I see skies of blue and clouds of white,
the bright blessed day,
The dark sacred night.
And I think to myself
What a wonderful world.

The colors of the rainbow

so pretty in the sky

are also on the faces

of people going by.

I see friends shaking hands

Saying "how do you do?"

They're really saying

I love you.

This song articulates where the bright lens takes me. When I look through this radical new lens, and see with my awakened eyes, I see a wonderful world. Despite the headlines, the wounds, the pain, and the fears. And I know God has told us, and emphasized, do not be afraid. I know we are directed to a shift of mind to put our emphasis on the goodness and love that is flowing. In doing so, we can create more and be witness to love expanding. This shift would honor this wonderful world and all of its glory.

Louis Armstrong was brought up in poverty, turmoil, faced discrimination and instability but could sing about a "wonderful world" from a place so deep within, from his soul. And he sang with a smile so big that it could light up the room.

Despite his childhood poverty, difficult upbringing, and the discrimination he encountered in his life, you could feel that he could still see love in people and a world of beauty and wonder. He sings with joy and makes me feel joy. Maybe, just maybe, this joy grew from his pain. I am also touched by the words recognizing that the simple gesture of a handshake is really a connection of souls and an expression of love. When your eyes are awakened you can catch, see, and feel more of the love as it flows from person to person, soul to soul. This bright lens allowed me to see the abundance of love being exchanged. It is being exchanged in small, simple ways like greetings and handshakes. And it is being exchanged in big, world-changing ways by people and organizations quietly going about their missions.

To conclude this story, I want to visit another poem in the book *The Prophet* by Kahlil Gibran. This poem is titled "On Joy and Sorrow." It is interesting that he lumps them together and, in the poem, he explains why. In the poem, he states: "Your joy is your sorrow unmasked." He goes on to say, "The deeper that sorrow carves into your being, the more joy you can contain." He then says "But I say unto you, they are inseparable. Together they come, and when one sits alone with you at your board, remember that the other is asleep upon your bed."

Each and every one of us holds masked sorrow, it is the essence of the human experience. Inner work leads you to release the grasp it holds. When the hardship begins to unravel, underneath this dark mask of sorrow, the bright lens will begin to shine and unveil the joy that lies within. My prayer is that if your mask remains in place, you can believe joy is there waiting. My hope is that the symbol of the bright lens can stir the emotions that will guide you to slumber more of the sorrow. When it is the joy that is sleeping, I hope the lens can guide you to awaken it. There will be times when you will be revisited and sitting alone with your sorrow. During these times when the burden is getting deeper from the carving of sorrow, allow the lens to remind you that you are increasing your capacity to be filled with joy. We go back to the Bible verse where we began:

> "May the God of hope fill you with all joy and peace as you trust in him that you may overflow with hope by the power of the Holy Spirit." - Romans 15:13

May that container carved from sorrow become filled with all joy and peace and be overflowing with the hope that only tremendous faith in the God of hope, feeding the wolf of love, and the power of the Holy Spirit can provide. With these things, the power lies within you to shift your mind and choose the bright lens. When you do, you will find, see, and become the grace that will lead you to be filled with hope and joy!

The Symbol

Miracles await when you
look to your heart where pure love resides.
That attention alone can completely
change the ebb of the winds and tides.

There is a lens available to center
on love and shift a fearful mind.
When you can see love is there
hope and miracles you will find.

This lens tells a story that love is in
your pain and love is in your sorrow.
When you believe love is there, you are
wiser and feel the hope held in tomorrow.

Imagine the possibilities when you see each
situation as leading you to learn.
Choose to look at the brighter side of life at
every new bend, twist and turn.

Imagine the possibilities where in each challenge
you look for the presence and flow of amazing grace.
Seeing life in this way can take you to a new,
refreshing and adventurous place.

A bright lens can soften
and open the burdened, blocked heart.
This change can transform your fearful mind
and create a new awakened start.

So, wear them literally or figuratively and experience your mind and perception shift. Give yourself, your world, and the world around you a joyous and miraculous lift!

Author's Note

Please know that I realize there are people in this world living in horrid conditions and understandably experience terror and fear daily. My intention for this book is to invite and encourage people to direct their thoughts to see and put more focus on the solutions and goodness in the world. When you become this blessed grace, you are giving the world a gift. You are feeding the wolf of love and spreading and sharing that bounty. In doing so, we might find, bring, and be hope to those suffering places. I believe there are solutions that are working and right before our eyes, and the bright lens can bring them to focus and expand the reach. The message from all the great spiritual authors and teachers that led my journey is that our combined thoughts are the collective energy that creates our world and makes it turn. My experience taught me what you plant and feed grows bigger. This works collectively as well as individually. Imagine the possibilities of more and more people truly awakening and beginning to view the world through this illuminating lens of light. This would mean our collective thoughts would come more from our connected souls and less from the ego, more from love and less from fear.

Albert Einstein is quoted as saying, "No problem can be corrected at the same level of consciousness from which it was created." All of our world's challenges were created at the level of ego and fear, the fear of not having enough or not being enough. This means our solutions are waiting to be realized at the level of awareness, compassion, and love. With this understanding, we can be open to recognize and cultivate leaders who are coming from an awakened place so that they may lead us to the solutions at a higher level.

I am so grateful that you found my book. I hope this new lens helps you as it did me to see the brightness in the world and that it brings you to metanoia, optimism, grace, and peace. And in these things, that you will be filled with hope and joy!

Humbly,

Marcia Fackler

Acknowledgements

> "Employ your time in improving
> yourself by other men's writings so that
> you shall come easily by what others
> have labored hard for."

Socrates

The inspiration for this book came through my practical nature. If the most practical and profound lessons that were sent to me through incredible grace could be merged, united, and combined in a simple, direct message, maybe it could reach and speak to many. As a seeker, I developed an insatiable hunger in the search for answers, purpose and truth. I read all

I could get my hands on from many authors I consider to be wise teachers, the ones mentioned and quoted in the story and many others. All I read became a part of me, and when these written words ignited sparks of insight, they became etched in my heart. I did my best to name and give credit where credit is due. But if words flow from me, that were sent to me and became part of me without memory of where they originated, it is not intentional. With all of my heart, I must acknowledge and express my gratitude to God, for the divine guidance I received in sending me these words and lessons when I needed them most and in delivering the inspiration to unite and bring them together.

I am forever grateful to the many authors and spiritual teachers who labored and whose works over the years have influenced and guided this journey. I tried to learn important life lessons through the labors and experiences of others as well as my own. I am eternally grateful to have received your wisdom and hopeful that by sharing it in this way, it brightens others' life path as it has my own.

Next, I must acknowledge the incredible support and confidence from my loving husband and partner in life, Steve.

He fulfilled every promise we made on that day in May, forty-eight years ago and has been a source of friendship, laughter, fun, stability, and security in the life of our family. I have always admired and appreciated his integrity and sense of responsibility. Our love has evolved and grown just as we have. Through all of the bumps and forks in our road, there was a map leading us, and together we followed it, side by side. Steve was the first to tell me that I viewed circumstances through rose-colored glasses, and I am forever grateful to him for inspiring this tool that became my important guiding symbol.

Becoming a mother is a magnificent teacher of love. I am enormously grateful for this gift and our 4 amazing children, Dustin, Adam, Ryan, and Hilary that have taught me so much. And, through those lessons, have given me so much. I continue to learn from and with them. A special thanks to Ryan, for following me along this road, encouraging me and for spending time going through the manuscript with me. In another poem from Kahlil Gibran's book *The Prophet* titled "On Children," he states: "Your children are not your children. They are the sons and daughters of Life's longing for itself. They come through you but not from you." I am forever grateful that Life's longing brought us together and for how they enriched my life. And I am so grateful that our circle of love continues to grow with the addition of 3 fabulous in-laws, Johanne, Emily, and John and the beautiful, amazing blessing of 11 grandchildren.

I must acknowledge and thank the 2 wonderful people, my mother and father—Roger and Milly Holzknecht—that brought me into this world and are no longer of this world. They were of the greatest generation who gave and sacrificed so much and on whose shoulders I stand. I hold the ideals of enormous respect, high integrity, loving patience, sacrifice, and hard work that they instilled and lived. It is my intention to pass it on and carry it forward. I am so grateful my mother encouraged and saw the benefits of an opened mind. My siblings Kent Holzknecht, Debbie Owen, and Donna Borntraeger were all an integral part of that foundation formed that our parents built, and we are the beneficiaries. Everyone that married into our family became remarkable bonus siblings— my sister-in-law Joan Holzknecht and brothers-in-law that are no longer with us, Tom Owen and Tom Borntraegeer. I am also so blessed to have the family that I married into. Dorothy, Al, and Jimmy Fackler who are no longer with us, Linda

Oliver, Denny Fackler, Phil and Laura Fackler and Lisa and Jerald Lewellen. They have always felt like family and been a significant part of my life. A special thanks to Lisa for being one of the first to share in this project with me and giving me her valuable input and sharing her thoughts.

This ordinary woman was extremely blessed with so many extraordinary friends! I can't imagine traveling the journey of life without the love and friendship of Jane Hebert, Linda Gleis, Karen Knight, Jan Woock, and Martha Dick. We were counselors, therapists, advisers, mentors, and confidantes for each other that, together, provided the wisdom and strength needed to make life better and just a little easier to navigate. We shared and went through so many of life's challenges and wonderful celebrations together. Together is always better. These strong, powerful women were a big influence in opening my mind and the grace that followed.

Life blessed me with an abundance of great friends, all whose love and presence has been a driving force for good in my life. There are lifelong friends with strong bonds formed through my kids, high school lifelong friends, work friends, Steve's high school friends, and neighborhood friends. They are all a tremendous blessing and add such a quality and sweetness to life.

My gratitude runs deep for another of my spiritual guides, Fr. Lawman Chibundi. He brings the gospels to life with his wisdom and insight. He inspired me with his courage and used his challenging life experiences to gain this wisdom that he shares with his congregation. What a light and blessing he is!

Alexis Mack came into my life, and we both believe it was through divine orchestration and a connection destined by God. She is my hero, my inspiration, and a guiding force. Our relationship began with me as the mentor, but I gained a wealth of personal growth from her as an example and by witnessing how she lives her life. She lives through selflessness, service, gratitude, courage, and humility. She is a rock for her family, a blessing for our community, and a light for our world. I am forever grateful that God brought us together and what having her in my life has taught me.

I must acknowledge all the selfless, strong women who worked tirelessly to keep the doors of Dress for Success Louisville open, which are too many to mention. And all of the inspiring women who came through the doors. As one wise client who joined the staff, named Morgan, said "I learned to have the mind of a student. Everybody you meet has something to teach you." The lessons I learned from all of them have been invaluable. I am so blessed to have had the opportunity to be in their presence and to serve. Nothing inspires me more than to witness a dimmed light begin to shine forth from the power within! I am privileged and honored to have been a witness.

A portion of the proceeds from sales of this book will be donated to Dress for Success Louisville. If you are in need of services, would like to make additional donations or become involved through volunteering they can be reached at:

Dress for Success Louisville

2722 Crittenden Drive

Louisville, Ky. 40209

502-584-8050

louisville.dressforsuccess.org

I am so grateful to the Fedd Books team that saw possibility in the story, pulled more of it out of me, and guided me through it all. Without them, it would never have been possible.

All these people taught, influenced, inspired, and were a part of this story that unfolded. They all contributed and brought me joy. How very blessed I am to have had all of them in my life to walk alongside of me and help me create this story. And, how blessed I feel to have lived it and to have the opportunity to send it forth and to share it.

References

Albert Einstein quoted by "Albert Einstein: What He Did and Didn't Say," Exploring Your Mind. Last update: July 28, 2022.

Alcoholics Anonymous, Alcoholic Anonymous, Fourth Addition, (New York: Alcoholics Anonymous World Services, Inc., 2001), 59

Ann Voskamp, *One Thousand Gifts: A Dare to Live Fully Right Where You Are* (Nashville, TN: Thomas Nelson, 2011)

Anne Frank, *Anne Frank's Tales from the Secret Annex: A Collection of her Short Stories, Fables, and Lesser-Known Writings* (New York: Bantam, 2003)

C.G. Jung, *Modern Man in Search of a Soul* (San Diego, CA: Harcourt Brace, 1955)

Cherokee Parable, Two Wolves

Dan O'Grady, quoted by Center for Action and Contemplation, "Turning Toward the Good." Richard Rohr Daily Meditation: Thursday, February 18, 2016 Titled - Turning Toward the Good.

Don Fogelberg, "The Wild Places," *The Wild Places*, Sony Music Entertainment, 1990, track 2, *Spotify*, https://open.spotify.com/album/0ivbe8Z9hLOViKscYEw2hi

Eckhart Tolle, *The Power of Now: A Guide to Spiritual Enlightenment* (Novato, CA: New World Library, 2004).

Eckhart Tolle, *A New Earth: Awakening to Your Life's Purpose* (New York: Penguin, 2008)

"The Eight Core Principles of the Center for Action and Contemplation," The Center for Action and Contemplation, Accessed July 18, 2023 https://cac.org/about/the-eight-core-principles/

Elpo, Definition from "Greek/Hebrew Definitions," BibleTools.org, accessed on July 21, 2023, https://www.bibletools.org/index.cfm/fuseaction/Lexicon.show/ID/G1680/elpis.htm

"Fight-or-Flight Response," psychologytools.com.

Gary Zukav, *The Seat of the Soul* (Saddle River, NJ: Prentice Hall & IBD (Reprint), 1989)

Gregory Boyle, *Tattoos on the Heart: The Power of Boundless Compassion* (New York: Free Press, 2011)

Helen Schucman, A Course in Miracles (West Sedona, AZ: Circle of Atonement, 2017)

John Lennon, "Imagine," *Imagine*, Remastered 2010, EMI Records Ltd, 1971, track 1, *Spotify*, https://open.spotify.com/album/0xzaemKucrJpYhyl7TltAk

Kahlil Gibran, "On Love," *The Prophet*, (New York: Alfred Knopf Inc., 1942), 11, 12

Kahlil Gibran, "On Joy and Sorrow," *The Prophet*, (New York: Alfred Knopf Inc., 1942), 29, 30

Kahlil Gibran, "On Children," *The Prophet*, (New York: Alfred Knopf Inc., 1942), 17

Lisa Miller, *The Awakened Brain: The New Science of Spirituality and Our Quest for an Inspired Life* (Manhattan: NY: Random House, 2021)

Louis Armstrong, "What a Wonderful World," What a Wonderful World, GRP Records Inc., 1968, track 1, *Spotify*, https://open.spotify.com/album/6mmv0gwumlFGWDGJXF4yEv

Mark Twain, AZQuotes.com

Marianne Williamson, *A Return to Love: Reflection on the Principles of a Course in Miracles* (San Francisco, CA: HarperOne, 1996)

Muhammed Ali, AZQuotes.com

Meister Eckhart, *Meister Eckhart: Selected Writings*, trans. Oliver Davies (New York: Penguin Books, 1994), 246-247.

Peter Mutabazi, *Now I Am Known: How a Street Kid Turned Foster Dad Found Acceptance and True Worth* (Ada, MI: Baker Books, 2022) 78, 79.

Repent, Definition from "To Live is to Change," Center for Action and Contemplation, January, 01, 2024, https://cac.org/daily-meditations/to-live-is-to-change/#:~:text=In%20this%20New%20Year's%20homily,a%20species%20are%20attracted%20to.

Richard Rohr, *Richard Rohr: Essential Teachings on Love,* ed. Joelle Chase and Judy Traeger (Ossining, NY: Orbis, 2018)

Sarah Ban Breathnach, *Simple Abundance: A Daybook of Comfort and Joy* (New York: Grand Central Publishing, 2019)

Thomas Merton, quoted by James Martin, *Becoming Who You Are: Insights on the True Self from Thomas Merton and Other Saints* (Mahwah, NJ: Paulist Press, 2006).

"Transforming Pain." Center for Action and Contemplation; Richard Rohr Daily Meditation: Wednesday, October 17, 2018.

Wayne Dyer, *The Power of Intention* (Carlsbad, CA: Hay House Inc., 2005)

Sin, thewordorigin.com